SOIL

Tim Cresswell was born in Cambridge in 1965 but didn't stay there long. Since then he has travelled, first as part of an Air Force family and then as a student and academic. As a geographer he is the author of five books on place, mobility and other key ideas in geographic thought. Since 2006 he has been Professor of Human Geography at Royal Holloway, University of London. He lives with his wife and three children in Acton, west London, but in 2013 they are relocating to Boston where Tim will transform into Professor of History and International Affairs at Northeastern University. *Soil* is his debut collection of poems.

Soil

Tim Cresswell

Penned in the Margins

LONDON

PUBLISHED BY PENNED IN THE MARGINS
Toynbee Studios, 28 Commercial Street, London E1 6AB
www.pennedinthemargins.co.uk

First published 2013

Printed in the United Kingdom by Bell & Bain Ltd.

ISBN
978-1-908058-15-7

CONTENTS

The Fox and the Skyscraper   11

A Glass of Water   13

Phase Shift   14

Rowan   15

Rare Metallophytes   17

First Snow   18

Dogfish   19

Human Geography I   21

Volunteers   23

Littoral   25

Myxamatosis, 1970s   27

Wormwood Jam   28

Human Geography II   29

Woman as Landscape   31

Parakeets   32

Earthwork   33

The Chicago Sound   34

Finding Karen Solie   35

Footnote   36

Soil   37

On entering the home of the bourgeois intelligentsia

                                    for the first time   64

Escape Plan   66

Avoid Disappointment   67

Possible Pubs   68

Metaphors   69

Suspicious Packages   70

Feverfew   71

Questions   72

Human Geography III   73

Turn   75

City Break   77

Human Geography IV   78

Synesthesia   79

Acknowledgements

Some of these poems (or close relatives) have appeared in *Agenda, Envoi, The Frogmore Papers, The North, Obsessed with Pipework, Stride* and *The Rialto*. 'Feverfew' appeared in the anthology *Herbarium* (Capsule Press, 2011). Three poems are featured in a special issue of *The Geographical Review* (April 2013) focusing on 'creative geographies'. Many thanks to Stan Dragland for editorial work on these poems.

I am very grateful for a wonderful cast of characters who have been instrumental in providing guidance and inspiration. These include Daljit Nagra, Barry Dempster, Susan Wicks, Philip Gross and, most of all, Jo Shapcott. My fellow travellers have provided continuous supportive but critical voices which have improved these poems no end. These include Liz Bahs, Amy Cutler, Sarah de Leeuw, Edward Doegar, Jemima Fincken, Irene James, Anja Koenig, Jo Lilley, Rebecca Morrison, Kate Potts, Julia Reckless, Richard Scott, Marek Urbanowicz and Clair Wilcox. Hats off to Tom Chivers whose editorial work made be feel more like myself 80 percent of the time. I could not ask for a better editor. Finally, thanks to my family for their support and bafflement in equal measure.

Soil

The Fox and the Skyscraper

Oh fox, in Japan they speak of *Kitsune*,
with nine full bushy tails, who waited
one hundred years to turn into a woman,
a beautiful lover to encounter alone
in the twilight. And in Arkansas,
Uncle Remus wove yarns of the trickster,
Bre'r Fox, who mixed tar with cloth
to fool a rabbit. Here we sing you,
oh *Reynardine*, the ware-fox, who wandered
late with shining teeth, luring
farmers' daughters to his castle
in the mountains. And the nameless fox
who went out on a winter's night
and prayed to the moon
to give him light before he reached
the town-o. And the fox who ran
as fast as he could and caught and ate
the gingerbread man. And the fox
who couldn't get the highest,
sweetest grapes. And *Fox in Sox*!
And the fox in Southwark
who climbed the stairs and ladders
seventy-three storeys to
the top of the Shard, grazing
on half-eaten kielbasa and jellied
pork-pie crusts discarded

by the carpenters and glaziers,
and every fox cell in hairs, nose
and notched ear hummed
as he sat, exhausted, rank
as any fox, gazing
out across London.

A Glass of Water

They say this glass of London water passed through eight bodies
                                                    before mine.
Starting near Heathrow. A Sikh cabby. The morning shift.
Then teacher between classes, a young woman, Kiwi, fit to burst.
A Southall market seller, bagging mangoes and bitter gourd.
A man who lives on a Brentford boat, pissing straight into the
                                                    Thames.
Kevin, who drank six pints last night and has a killer thirst.
A gardener at Kew tending orchids, blooming just one day.
Carrie, just up from bed, still red-raw from energetic sex.
And old man Andy, up the road, downing morning pills.

They say my body is sixty percent this. Blood. Spit. Plasma. Piss.
A constant whoosh and sluice. Tidal. Tethered to the moon
like a walking, thinking sea. I half expect to stretch and flop —
a water balloon about to pop and drench my neighbour
on the Tube with my multitude of juices
in waves — six small splashes then a seventh monster —
enough to drown the Underground.

Phase Shift

A light turns on. Through a window a man in shorts is ironing —
two towers stand dark against the Acton evening —

red tiled roofs, terracotta chimney pots — a line of lights sinking
in strict tempo to Heathrow, beyond the spires and officeblocks.

The man is folding shirts, his life marked by the widespread
presence of mammals and flowering plants —

the rumble of a skateboard, the humdrum of cars on the Westway.
He is a geological force to be reckoned with.

The door closes behind him, the light still on. A cats creeps
along a walltop, across the road, down an alley. Sodium lights pop.

The street submits to echoes and foxes. In the morning
the dustbin men appear with their dayglo and intricate systems

in a place that could spend millions of years buried
and still blackbirds wake me up in spring,

in this city that reveals through crushed structures
that it is unlike melancholy, for instance.

Rowan

One spring of blossoms —
    pink petals littered the streets
        from our first floor window — then

they chopped down
    the cherry trees
        outside our house.

In from the hinterlands
    came Mountain Ash,
        Rowan —

municipal trees
    with feathered leaves
        and tight-fisted berries

for drunken birds to guzzle.
    Everywhere, they loiter
        unnoticed, ubiquitous,

filtering urban air.
    Tidy. Low maintenance.
        Respectful.

But think of them far north
    or at higher altitude,

red berries

against snow:
        all shamelessness
            and attitude.

Rare Metallophytes

Spring sandwort, alpine penny-cross,
mountain pansy: disaster lovers,
first on the scene of the misery
of ruptured earth, hanging on,
facing off, digging in. Coping
in the hinterlands of old lead mines.

Two months of cheerful, tufted
fuck-yous to the shafts and pylons left
by the dirt-encrusted hands and
steel-hard biceps of those who trucked off
the malleable metal for pistol shot,
roof flashing, batteries, radiation shields.

.

First Snow

Your skull was still inside your mother
as they twisted in a screw attached to
a wire attached to a monitor which re-
layed sounds of your heart racing, stalling
and then racing. I saw the blood
trickle down between her legs. The room smelled
of batteries, sweat. Low pressure brings on birth,
the midwife said, as if the snow outside
might suck you out.
                              I drive our old
duck-egg Volvo through the reconfigured
city — I am Scott or Amundsen —
the first man in an unmapped land longing
for trig points, the pole star in a cold sky,
the certainties of magnetic north.

Dogfish

Wanting whiting,
bream or bass,
the dogfish kept biting.

We reeled them in,
twisting and jerking,
enjoying the sport.

Once caught,
they're released in disgust.
They do not grace tables

at The Fat Duck,
garnished with space dust,
rhubarb or chocolate.

It's all sinewy flesh -
gelatinous muscle and cartilage —
not delicate sole

nor silky Halibut.
Part shark, part eel,
neither one nor both;

an in-between fish,
its skin feels like

coarse grain sandpaper

that can graze yours clean off.
So maligned,
treated as trash,

it travels under an alias —
Rock-Salmon or Huss —
but few of us are fooled.

Some mornings
when the fishermen have
upped sticks

bodies are found
gull-pecked
along the tidal zone,

carcasses thrown
carelessly about.
Evidence of hooks too deep

to disgorge.
Guts pulled out
through gasping mouths.

Human Geography I

I wake to the glow of LEDs and the murmur of Radio 4 — get up
naked in the gloom — a plane to catch — my clothes piled on the
landing, outside the room where my wife still sleeps — through the
lifting fog I brush teeth and down pills — past dreaming kids — a
hurried tea and toast — out the door to the blue light of a city half
awake.

I am familiar with airports — feel at home there — know their codes
and customs — I've learnt to read the signs — black on yellow —
the two colours with maximum contrast — easy to see and follow.
I stand in lines — know my place — unbuckle my belt — put my
shoes in plastic trays — reveal my identity — know the difference
between business and pleasure. I travel light with my MacBook Air
— check in online — know all the best seats — maximum pitch —
extra legroom — exit rows.

I'm comfortable in airports — stripped of all decision-making
powers — wile away the hours reading the business section or
reviews of books I ought to read — watching planes through plate
glass windows think of boyhood's *Observer's Book of Aircraft*.

Sometimes I think I'd like to stop — start relationships with sediments
— dry stone walls. Write about ravens or rivers of ice cracking in
glaciers. I want to hear nature sing — catch the ringing of a thrush
breaking snails on stones. These are just facts and things.

My plane is boarding — number's called. I heft my bag — get in line — show my passport one last time. Weightless — down the ramp into the plane and find my seat.

Volunteers

In
  between
    the certainties
      of paving stones

weeds have appeared.
  Someone, long ago,
    measured to the
      nearest centimeter

this yard, and chose
  which stones to lay.
    I fancy that they disagreed
      on shades of red and grey.

And then, for scent,
  they planted
    beds of lavender and
      climbing roses.

But now we're here
  and through the grout
    I see the rebel heads
      of dandelions,

bindweed, clover,

nettles and
who-knows-what?
begin to sprout.

And there
amongst them all
a familiar form
lies bent

under the weight
of seven green fruit —
and one quite red.
A tomato plant,

as unintended
as any weed,
muscles out the vagabonds
and volunteers its load.

Littoral

this

is where
the lugworms live   samphire grows
      water
      deposits
      its salt
crabs crawl side —
      ways
and dunes
      creep
        imperceptibly

old bottles for medicines
and ginger beer
     appear
      and disappear
saltmarsh
     bog bodies
        estuary mud

the negation of
      measurement
the invention of fractals

migrant birds

make temporary
homes

archaeology emerges
              old harbours
          inscrutable circles of stone

someone swore
they saw
the shadow of a ship

and twice a year
on the lowest tide
stumps and trunks
of petrified trees
bring rumours of
Atlantis!

Myxamatosis, 1970s

We found a rabbit —
crazy — lolloping
in the trees with
sightless eyes
in a swollen head.
The merciful thing
was to kill it.
Kick it hard or
bash its brains out.
We hung it
spinning from
a branch and hit it
with a stick —
sending it
into orbit,
till its body split
in two, spraying
a Catherine wheel
of blood and liquid
rabbit shit
that covered us
in reek and gunge
that stayed with us
for weeks.
This happened.
I was there.

Wormwood Jam

Before the devil pisses on berries.
Late September. Blackberrying down the
Scrubs — by high high helixes of razor
wire. Filling plastic peanut-butter pots
with blackred fruit. Brimfull. Soursharp. Inky.
Imploding sweet — squashed by over-eager
fingers — gashing hands on brambles that could
pull the wool from sheep. Gambling on low fruit
slashed on by Shepherds and Rottweilers.

The kitchen filled with blackberry. Cauldrons
of redblack boiling glop. I tried to catch
the setting point — risking burns and blisters —
my finger forming surface crinkles through
bloodthick syrup on a frozen saucer.

Human Geography II

Consider a woman walking down stairs. It's raining outside — tarmac glistens — it's cold for March — her head full of poems: mountains, food, and a lover she has lost. Many years together with dogs, recipes, music — walks they took — forests, islands, snow, desert sand by cactus plants — and the meals they shared — oh what meals, what perfect pumpkin soups, what farmhouse cheese, what singular oranges — and what salmon - especially salmon — fresh — smoked — salt as sea — sweet as toffee. Cookbooks bear the stains of chocolate, wine, tomatoes — fingerprints of life together.

A man sits at the bottom of the stairs drinking beer and smoking. He doesn't usually smoke but the rush of nicotine reminds him of a woman he once knew — a woman who could shake the rain out of the air. Together they had travelled. Once, after making love in a caravan in Spain, they had shared a shower — she had led him back to bed still wet, and made love to him again. This moment filled his life — he wanted it back.

Imagine lines around the world — his lines — her lines — traces of their lives. Their lines have crossed before in Amsterdam by the Rijksmuseum — in Bombay and San Francisco — in New York City somewhere on the Lower East Side. They have driven the Mississippi north. They have passed through JFK, ORD and LAX. They have been ticketed, photographed, fingerprinted, identified — welcomed through to airside. They have walked. Their feet have stepped over the shadows of chewing gum — stopped as they watched skateboarders flipping tricks — stumbled over curbs and cracks in pavements. Their feet have done hard miles in ill-fitting shoes, blistered, swollen in heat — urgent on Fifth Avenue, cacophonous in Seoul, languid in Lisbon. As they walk they take little bits of places with them — they cut desire lines across the grass. They have pressed themselves upon the earth and the earth is different now.

Woman as Landscape

Listen. I know it's wrong to conflate
the female body with land
what with all the history that's freighted with
but there was this woman on the radio
who said she had a landscape
imprinted on her heart.

Now, I'm no cartographer but I liked — no, *loved* —
this woman's voice —
from somewhere near a different sea —
and as I made my coffee
I saw the soil in her blood swooshing along
with the clotting agents and hemoglobin
and roads marked out from synapse to synapse,
conglomerations gathering behind her knees;
main streets of half-abandoned cowboy towns
with saloon doors and dust devils jammed
between her toes, twin cantinas with three
kinds of homemade salsa right behind her nipples.

I thought of her waking to the squeek of a swinging
stoplight, local radio buzzing in her ears,
paper mills and marsh gas flickering in her eyes.

I'm sure she knows the names of birds.

Parakeets

Forty of you were released
during the filming of *The African Queen*,
or maybe by Jimi Hendrix!
Rumours. In any case,
you're a new entry among the top twenty
garden birds of Britain, dashingly
integrating with blackbirds and blue tits.
                    Your green tails
flash from tree to tree between Ealing chimneys.
We hear you, gathered in gangs, calling
and squawking along the oak branches of Acton.
                    Watch it —
they've got it in for you, fearing the displacement
of woodpeckers, nuthatches and starlings,
the 'alien invasive' starlings introduced to Central Park,
NYC, along with every bird mentioned in Shakespeare.
                    There's talk
of a cull. For my part, I hope the colour
and screech of Mysore and Mogadishu
does not dwindle into cartographic memory
like smallpox and the Roman Empire.

Earthwork

I walk along the river path, stamping
puffballs underfoot, catching the deathscent
of rot and earthmusk. Squeezing juniper
berries — unearthing perfect London gin.
The rustle of a squirrel's tail — redtingedblack
brings me back to a river in Alberta.
Across the Bow — the delvethrust rock
and roll of scrumpled sedimentary
earthrock.   Accordianed.
          Curtainpleated.
Folded on
          eroded
                    energetic land.
Slow.   Work.

Being less Wordsworth and more flâneur, earth
leaves me small. Approaching campus I'm met
by opera
          trills climbing
                    toppling over
the lowbuzzhum of generators.

Behind the studios mud is earthscraped
by bucketteeth. Islands of new chocolate mulch.
Sudden topography! Opera in E flat!
Flatearth and mudmuck. Quickwork.

The Chicago Sound

I'm out of joint, jet-lagged,
speaking with an accent.
Towers swarm
with the hum of
a million air conditioners —
ventilation shafts throwing
condensation columns
high into the firmament.
And traffic on Michigan Avenue hums
base notes for the retro metal squeal
and screech of trains
on the rickety Meccano contraption
of the elevated railway.
Helicopter throbs — chops the
air looking for snags and hold-ups.
A plane climbs out of O'Hare.
Its engines whine and strain
as it describes its rising
arc and strikes out north over
Lincoln Park along
the shore towards
permafrost and silence.
Even sirens sound exotic —
as though trauma demands
a dialect
as local as birdsong.

Finding Karen Solie

I lost myself in bigspace rhythms
    trailer-trash
    back-seat sex
vast prairies punctuated
        with two-bit motels
        diner coffee
        broken lives
    the edges of boreal forests
        unsuccessful fucks
           rusting boats
              bruised waitresses
                drunken men in pick-up trucks

lines piling up — words falling off the edge of the page

it was ready to be
    stamped with DATE DUE BACK

        blank as a prairie
           from an airplane
        an unused bed
    I took it out to
        bend corners
           thumb edges.

Footnote

Foot.[1] Note.[2]

---

[1] A term used in poetics to describe the rhythm of things
— the beat of sounds
the end of limbs
the bearer of weight
an archaic unit of measurement
our attachment to the earth

[2] A reminder
a command to pay attention
a small sheet of paper
currency — a high denomination
a term used in music to describe a single sound
— its pitch and its duration

Soil

Soil is a historico-geological notion.
Michel Foucault

1

the A horizon — topsoil — rich in the litter of leaves twigs carapaces
earthworms — a shallow bed of minerals and moisture

the B horizon — this is the heart of the matter — the material used
for classification by pedologists — the location of a soil's identity

the C horizon consists of weatherized rocks   becoming   soil

bedrock — the parent material — a strong influence on soil
development

2

Were (God) created earth
out of three soil types
      black top soil
      red middle soil
      white bottom soil

then he fashioned black people from black soil
then he fashioned brown people from red soil
then he fashioned white people from white soil

3

digging a hole in the garden
I noticed the lines of white

                        the chalk
the chalk that made the white horse at Uffington
where we tried to fly our kites

giant chalk mines
quarried with matchbox cars

battalions of the eighth army
glad to be out of the sand

4

autochthony
(auto = self + chthon = soil)
born of the soil
from here and irreducibly so
mortals made from earth
possessing the land that birthed us
not driving others out
not arriving and finding it empty
not mixing in motley hordes
        Athenians
noble   pure
soil sprung
our land is nurse   mother   father   midwife

I met a woman on a plane
and as we cruised at 36,000 feet over Nevada
she told me she was from a tribe in the Pacific Northwest
she told me of the myths
the scientist made up
the landbridge
the arrival
from the steppes and ice
of Eurasia

5

worms and water filter down
mixing organic matter with
                        minerals
materials bleed
        vertically
        through
        leaching
in the B horizon as water drips
                    down
                    through
                    ground
like coffee

6

cloying dark lumpy soil
sticking to boots
as he squatted in the sugar beet
to drink his cold tea

sometimes dad would
wipe a crusted globe
with his frozen hand
and bite into it
     raw
to taste the sugar

retch on the mouthful
of Norfolk dirt

7

Soil. First there was just this —
this and the rain.

And then cum from Athena's thigh
wiped with wool and tossed

away. A million blind whiplash
cells in a sugary sea

swarming through the leaf litter,
mingling with nematodes

and fungal spores — DNA
and minerals.

Soil began to spin
brown flurries, becoming

columns. Centrifugal
forces molded sand and clay —

rims and rivulets made
by no hands.

Limbs from clay and sand —
fingers, nose, teeth,

earlobes — cracks and flaps beneath
the folding gut

Ericthonius — autochthonous
soil born — Athenian.

8

loose   noncoherent   falls apart when dry or moist

friable   easily crushed   forms into lumps

firm   resistance is distinctly noticeable

plastic   forms a wire when rolled between thumb and forefinger

sticky   adheres to other material

cemented   water runs across it

hard   broken with difficulty

soft   powders with slight pressure

9

the material in the B horizon usually
derives from
the C horizon and is thus local

translocation
    of materials from the A horizon occurs
as worms and other organisms
                move deeper

B horizons
    have subscripts which indicate what materials
have moved and mingled
Bh   for instance   indicates
          the presence of humus – rich organic matter

10

Is this what you did? Was it this, mother?
up at night, out in the garden
gorging on ferrous earth, shoveling hands
into raised beds; clods and clumps between your
toes, feeling the clay wick the wet away
from the membranes in your mouth
streaks of mud on the hem of your
nightie in the morning. Did you scrub your
nails till your skin was raw?

I find myself standing under an orange moon,
face smeared with rich loam, fish blood and bone,
wondering how I got here.

11

boundaries
              between
horizons
are often
   mixed up
      merged
churned by worms
    and other organisms

deep roots
           of oaks and ash cut down though
the B horizon tapping nutrients
                          ensuring drainage

12

An ti go   a soil to know
Wisconsin's crops and livestock grow
and forests too   on An ti go
and forests too   on An ti go[1]

---

[1]   The Antigo Silt Loam song extolls the virtues of the state soil of Wisconsin. It was written by the soil scientist — F.D. Hole. Sections 15 & 18 also derive from this song.

13

remember Wisconsin
where you whisked me out to Devil's Lake
to celebrate
and fucked me
amongst the birch
on that tartan travel rug
my fingers in the leaf mould
soil under my nails
surrounded by
the fungal scent
of earth and sex

14

loess (not loss, not lust) —
deposits of silt that have been left by the wind
Aeolian
      loose stuff
         blown across the earth

slightly coherent dust

some forms at the end of large glaciers
                      from the floodplains
of braided
   glacial streams
   that dry out in the winter
leaving finely ground deposits to be picked up
by the wind
        tossed and deposited
along the Mississippi
at Crowley's Ridge in Arkansas
      for instance

15

great Lakes region
fertile land
you strengthen us
in heart and hand
each slope
      each flower
            each wild bird call
proclaims a
  unity
in all

16

many soils have Russian names like *Podzol*
     and *Chernozem*
Chernozem means 'black' (from Russian *chern*)
and 'earth' (from Russian *zemlja*)
black   earth
Zemlja means 'earth' but also 'land'
black   land

not wanting Russians to have all the names
(this was the Cold War, after all)
Chernozem
    became
     Mollisol
in the United States Department of Agriculture Soil Taxonomy

17

bedrock
is only one influence on soil type
things move
drainage
  run-off
      swamp hollows
animals
us

18

plant a seed
and pull a weed
the soil will give us
all we need
and plenty more
so birds may feed
so birds may feed
  birds may feed
    birds may feed
soil will give so
    birds may feed
pull a weed
  so birds may feed
and plenty more so
  birds may feed

19

the Nazis spoke of 'blood and soil'
both can be rich in iron
soil rich
    in iron looks
            brown
or even red

20

sand
  loamy sand
          sandy loam
loam
   silt loam
 silt
   sandy clay loam
             clay loam
                 silty clay loam
            sandy clay
      silty clay
clay

21

at the Rocky Mountain Arsenal
in Commerce City   Colorado
they made nerve gas
contaminating soil with
aldrin
isodrin
dieldrin
dibromochloropropane (DBCP)
diisopropylmehylphosphate (DIMP)
p-chlorophenylmethylsulfoxide (PCPMSO)
and arsenic

all disposed of in unlined graves

22

areas
with clay soils
produce
dullness
and stupidity

23

geophagy
(geo = earth + phagy = eating)

has been observed in the American South
among pregnant women who prefer
    red clay earth which is rich
in iron

24

somewhere
there is a woman who is mad
madly in love
she wakes up early to tend her allotment
her little patch of London earth
as the sun comes up in a blueing sky
she reaches down and weeps
into the soil which she shovels
into her mouth   feeling it dry
as the clay wicks the wet away
feeling the grit and the crack
of gravel and woodlice between
her teeth

On entering the home of the bourgeois intelligentsia for the first time

1984
       huge house in North Oxford
           paintings gathering dust
unhung on the floor
paintings I didn't   understand
stairs
    used
        to store
           books
kitchen table never   cleared
— things pushed   aside
       to make
       a place to eat
       plates didn't   match
       neither did   mugs
coffee made in percolators
       like in France   it was thick
and strong
salad before   dinner
piles
       everywhere
       and everything looked
       important
chairs had stories and never seemed to be replaced
book-lined studies

                    enough books
to take a
lifetime
to read
                    enormous windows

Then and there I wanted to be like that.
To live in a house of careless piles.
For the furniture not to match.
To drink coffee out of bowls
and have salad before dinner.
Olive oil and vinegar.
Vast sprigs of rosemary on chunks of lamb.
Paintings, not prints, in every room hung
                                randomly. Books
e   v   e   r   y   w   h   e   r   e.

Old oriental rugs, careworn and threadbare.
And I would wear crumpled linen and throw dinner parties
at the d
        r
        o
            p
of a h

        a

        t.

Escape Plan

If the cold doesn't kill me and I can hold my breath
like any Blue Whale and velocity
doesn't wrench my arms
from my body
and the shock
doesn't make
my heart
stop
then I can
skydive
spiraling
left and right
picking my
spot to
make an
entry:
arrow
straight
feet
together
barely
a splash
ten
out
of
ten

Avoid Disappointment

and while you're at it, circumnavigate
sadness. Aim low. Hedge your bets.
Start with high quality ingredients.
Always accept second best. Don't let
the occasional lemon sour your
experience. Make sure your tickets
are authentic. Double check!
Do not expect anything from anyone.
Suspend disbelief. Hire a detective.
Practice an aversion to theory. Leave plenty
of time for travel to and from your
destination. Make lists. Keep them
short. Book early.

Possible Pubs

meet me	at the rush and shiver
take me	to the pat and tap
meet me	at the pluck and quiver
take me	to the tickle and clap
seek me	by the curve and flutter
find me	in the wince and snide
seek me	by the trust and stutter
find me	in the pulse and slide
see me	at the luck and couple
join me	near the kiss and skew
see me	at the curse and suckle
join me	near the wreck and screw
hold me	in the wrench and stare
drink with me love	drink with me there

Metaphors

The central controller of the Athens public transport service is in charge of metaphors. She decides what is connected and what remains separate. Some of her favourites are rollercoaster to stock exchange, home to castle and brothel to meat market. The passengers are happy — they know where to get on and where to get off. They recognize the route. Recently, however, she started to get bored and play with her maps. Doodling with consequences. On Monday she drew a line from the brothel to the hospital, disconnecting the meat market in the process. On Tuesday the meat market and the zoo were connected. The complaints started to arrive. On Wednesday a train left the parliament building and stopped at the party shop leaving passengers bewildered. On Thursday she considered a Parthenon to Pireus line — all those old columns to sailors and the sea. Too obvious! Instead the post office was linked with the prison. By the end of the week it was possible to get a non-stop direct metaphor from the art gallery to the abattoir — from the place where she was spent to the spot where she counted her blessings. Confused by this sudden change in transport planning, people started to make their own connections — sometimes even walking.

Suspicious Packages

Look left and right when crossing the road.
Never openly look at maps in strange cities;
avoid alleyways at night.

Never fly on airlines from places where you can't drink the water;
if a man with a knife asks you for your wallet — give it to him.
Remove bones from fish with tweezers
        and take the skin off the breasts of chickens.

Abstain from holidays in countries with a history of landmines.
Pay attention to the latest advice of doctors and the Foreign Office.
Always have at least one glass of red wine a day
        and never more than three.

Seek the safety of crowds;
bend your knees when lifting heavy objects;
stay away from the edges of cliffs, fast-flowing rivers
        and shifting sands.

Do not be a hero.
Do not have unprotected sex with strangers.
Do not approach a dead bird on the pavement.

Pay attention to suspicious packages.

Feverfew

Snakeroot   Rainfarn

            Febrifuge
Ague Plant
                    Maid's Weed
                            Bachelor's Button
                                    Nose Bleed
            Pyrethrum

    Mutterkraut
            Altamisa
                        Flirtwort
                            Manzanilla

            Feather foil
Wild   Chamomile

Questions

from Lord Randal, *Child Ballad 12*

All these fucking questions. Where have I been?
What did I do? Who did I meet? Enough!
D'you want this blue-eyed son to scram, to dream
of disappearance, run far, fall in love
with my cousin? You treat me like a kid
who's never glimpsed the ocean. I'm thirty-
three. Six foot two. I've shared the dirtied beds
of whores. Never met a fist that hurt me.

Last night I ate with my tower-block lover:
mushrooms and shellfish, sour red berries,
confessing that I had loved another
in the frost and freeze of January.
My stomach's churning — make my bed soon —
stop all these questions — I have to lie down.

Human Geography III

My love moves through the house alone. She empties the cat litter
— lines the compost bin with Saturday's *Guardian* — folds the
children's clothes. She puts lists on the fridge and post-it notes inside
which read "always wrap the cheese!" She moves the knife from
the counter's edge. She writes a note to school and makes a call to
arrange a birthday party. There are always envelopes in the bureau
— I have not bought envelopes since I can't remember when. She
does the work of love, of maintenance.

I am elsewhere. I am not there.

She is the Queen of Entropy. She notices decay. The places where the
paint has chipped — the window frames need another coat — the
gaps between the floorboards where cork has crumbled letting cold
air in — the picture hung askew — the curtain where it ripped. She
broods over the dust on the baseboards, disappointed by the stains
the dishwasher leaves, surprised that the laundry bin is full again.

I am abroad. I am travelling.

Between tasks she thinks of other places. Honeymoon rickshaws
amongst the water buffalo — a fast-flowing stream near Uncle Ken's
Mount Mitchell — a bookshop in Dupont Circle — her dormroom at
Duke. She feels the sand on a beach on Cardigan Bay from where she
watched the dolphins. She hears the sadness of sheep and the rapid-
fire mew of the Kite.

I leave. I fly out. I take taxis.

Does she picture me in restaurants in Buenos Aires, Taipei, Chicago — conjure interesting people for me to talk to — see me in green hotel rooms — trace my lines of flight around the globe — place me in basements drinking beer? Does she sit me on the right-hand side of the aircraft so I spy our house on the descent into Heathrow?

Turn

after Tam Lin, *Child Ballad 39*

you can turn me in your arms

                into Jack-of-the-green

you can turn me in your arms

                into all-of-a-lather

you can turn me in your arms

                into change-in-the-weather

you can turn me in your arms

                three sixty degrees

you can turn me in your arms

                into froth and foam

you can turn me in your arms

                into the things that I said

you can turn me in your arms

                an expletive deleted

you can turn me in your arms

                into midnight moan

I will turn you in my arms

                into dervishing light

I will turn you in my arms

                into 2 x 3

I will turn you in my arms

                into whatever I please

I will turn you in my arms

                into extra time, a skipped beat

you can turn me in your arms

                                     into a naked man

hold fast and fear not

                                     I'll be myself again

City Break

The smart hotel in Lisbon
we ran to in foreign rain,

child-free and eager,
touching more, together,

duvet discarded, a new
city outside. Who'd have guessed

the whole shebang was on the verge
of economic ruin?

What mattered? Me inside you.
The absence of necessity.

Human Geography IV

Let's walk from Acton Main Line and the airport train down Horn Lane — dried out, jet-lagged - through morning air not yet tinged with disappointment — smell diesel and jet fuel from lorries and planes ascending west. Let's listen to the planes — the bass note rumble — the high whine of throttle-up — the idle rattle of queuing cars. Inhale cement-works dust. Pass the Africans outside Acton Cabs — the Polish delis with their unintelligible sausages — the cactus pears and passion fruit spilling out over the pavement — Sam's fried chicken and the pawn shop.

I don't stop — the world goes the other way as I come home. The end of something amongst all these beginnings. My desire lines collapse behind me as I come to the front door. The leaves need sweeping — there's litter in the hedgerow — cigarette butts, fast food boxes, crisp packets — salt and vinegar, someone's sock. Pages from the *Metro*.

Opening the door — chaos — the shoes fall out across the hall — the recycling is full — that crack that needs filling. Still. In my memory this place had attained some kind of order in my absence. There's breakfast dishes in the sink and still-warm coffee in the bottom of the mug.

Later I tell stories of travels — things tasted — conversations related approximately — gifts disgorged — an attempt to undersell perhaps — fighting jetlag — back into the swing of things — shopping — kids to school — make like I never left.

Synesthesia

I came. And in the interlude
she tells me she orgasmed
blue. Blue like movies? Blue like sad?
Is that why she cries sometimes?
Half asleep she shook her head.
No. Really. It was fine.

She sinks to sleep, leaving me
alone with the digital
green alarm glow and sodium
orange through the gaps around
the velux blinds. A late jumbo
throttles up and noses over Harlesden.